WHY WE EAT HEALTHY FOODS

by Rosalyn Clark

BUMBA BOOKS™

LERNER PUBLICATIONS ◆ MINNEAPOLIS

Note to Educators:

Throughout this book, you'll find critical thinking questions. These can be used to engage young readers in thinking critically about the topic and in using the text and photos to do so.

Lerner Publications Company
A division of Lerner Publishing Group, Inc.
241 First Avenue North
Minneapolis, MN 55401 USA

For reading levels and more information, look up this title at www.lernerbooks.com.

Library of Congress Cataloging-in-Publication Data

Names: Clark, Rosalyn, 1990– author.
Title: Why we eat healthy foods / Rosalyn Clark.
Description: Minneapolis : Lerner Publications, [2018] | Series: Bumba books.
  Health matters | Audience: Age 4–7. | Audience: K to grade 3. | Includes
  bibliographical references and index.
Identifiers: LCCN 2017026369 (print) | LCCN 2017021597 (ebook) | ISBN
  9781512482966 (eb pdf) | ISBN 9781512482935 (lb : alk. paper) | ISBN
  9781541511064 (pb : alk. paper)
Subjects: LCSH: Nutrition—Juvenile literature.
Classification: LCC RA784 (print) | LCC RA784 .C5315 2018 (ebook) | DDC
  613.2—dc23

LC record available at https://lccn.loc.gov/2017026369

Manufactured in the United States of America
3-52988-33140-3/22/2022

Expand learning beyond the printed book. Download free, complementary educational resources for this book from our website, www.lerneresource.com.

Table of Contents

Healthy Foods

There are so many different kinds

of food!

Healthy foods are good for you.

Which foods are healthy?

Fruits and vegetables are healthy.

They have vitamins.

Vitamins help your body stay strong.

Oranges are healthy.

They have vitamin C.

Vitamin C helps your body heal.

Can you name some other healthy fruits?

Carrots are healthy.

They have vitamin A.

Vitamin A helps keep your

eyes healthy.

Dairy foods are made

from milk.

Milk has calcium.

Calcium is good for

your bones.

Can you name any dairy foods?

Meat has protein.

So do nuts and beans.

Protein helps your

muscles grow.

Foods such as bread have grains.

Grains have fiber.

Fiber is good for your heart.

Foods such as eggs have fat.

Your body needs some fat.

Fat gives you energy.

Why do you think your body needs energy?

Many foods are healthy.

What healthy foods do you

like to eat?

Healthy Food Groups

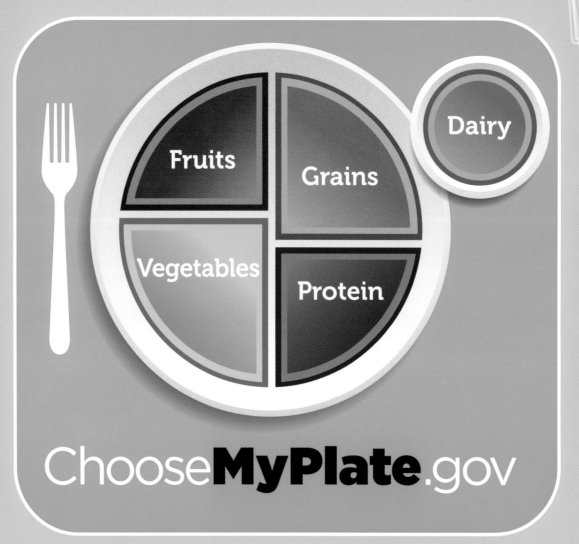

ChooseMyPlate.gov

Fruits, vegetables, grains, protein, and dairy products are healthy. We should eat them every day. This picture shows a balanced meal.

Picture Glossary

dairy

foods and beverages that are made from milk

fruits

sweet products of trees and plants that have seeds and can be eaten

grains

small, dry seeds that are made into food

vegetables

plants or products of plants that can be eaten

23

Read More

Bellisario, Gina. *Choose Good Food! My Eating Tips.* Minneapolis: Millbrook Press, 2014.

Boothroyd, Jennifer. *What's on My Plate? Choosing from the Five Food Groups.* Minneapolis: Lerner Publications, 2016.

Coan, Sharon. *Good for Me: Healthy Food.* Huntington Beach, CA: Teacher Created Materials, 2016.

Index

Photo Credits